D1518685

CHAPTER ONE

AN OBESE WORLD

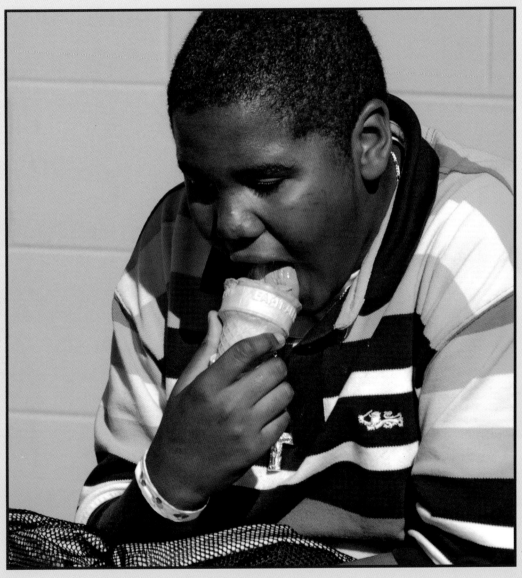

*To be obese, more than 30 percent of your body
weight must be composed of fat.*

TABLE OF CONTENTS

Published in the United States of America by Cherry Lake Publishing
Ann Arbor, Michigan
www.cherrylakepublishing.com

Content Advisor: Carolyn Walker, RN, PhD, Professor, School of Nursing, San Diego
State University, San Diego, California

Photo Credits: Cover and page 1, AP Images/Petros Giannakouris; page 4, © M. Stock/
Alamy; page 7, Maury Aaseng; page 9, © Press Association/Alamy; page 11, © Findlay/
Alamy; page 14, AP Images/Madaline Hebranko; page 17, AP Images/Ed Betz; page 19,
Shutterstock; page 21, © Ed Robles/Shutterstock; page 23, AP Images/Ed Betz; page 25,
© Pauline Cutler/Alamy; page 28, Alamy

Library of Congress Cataloging-in-Publication Data
Allman, Toney.
 Obesity / Toney Allman.
   p. cm.—(Health at risk)
Includes index.
ISBN-13: 978-1-60279-285-2
ISBN-10: 1-60279-285-2
1. Obesity—Juvenile literature. I. Title. II. Series.
RC628.A45 2008
616.3'98—dc22   2008017499

*Cherry Lake Publishing would like to acknowledge the work of
The Partnership for 21st Century Skills.
Please visit www.21stcenturyskills.org for more information.*

21st Century Skills Library

HEALTH AT RISK

OBESITY

Toney Allman

Cherry Lake Publishing
Ann Arbor, Michigan

*O*bese is not just another word for fat or **overweight**. If you are **obese**, that means about 30 percent of your weight, or more, is body fat. (The rest of your weight is called lean tissue. Lean tissue includes bones, muscles, and organs.) Pretend you are an adult. You're 5 feet 9 inches tall (1.75 m). A healthy weight for you is about 125 to 168 pounds (57 to 76 kg). If you weigh between 169 pounds (77 kg) and 202 pounds (92 kg), you're overweight. If you weigh more than 202 pounds (92 kg), you are obese. Today, lots of people weigh too much. It is a problem in many countries.

About one-third of adults in the United States and Canada are obese.

Learning & Innovation Skills

Feed your virtual pet doughnuts at Neopet. com. Add the King from Burger King to your friends list on MySpace. Enjoy a pro sports event sponsored by a soft drink company. Food companies make junk food and fast food seem cool. They do that by appealing to your emotions, not to your brain. Get smart. Experts say you can learn to tell the truth from the hype by asking yourself questions about products with a cool message: Who is sending the message? What is their goal? How is the message affecting you?

Obesity is a problem around the world, but it is worse in some countries than others. Japan, for example, has low rates of obesity compared with the United States or Canada. The typical Japanese diet includes mostly vegetables and fish. Refined foods such as white bread, white sugar, and sweet cereal are not part of the diet. Fatty oils and meats are not common either. In cities, Japanese people walk to work and school or walk to catch buses and trains. However, when Japanese people switch to Western lifestyles, they are less likely to follow these healthy habits. They buy cars and drive instead of walking. They eat fatty and refined foods. They learn to like fast foods. Then, they become overweight just as Americans do.

About 17 percent of children and teens in the United States and Canada are obese, too. Many more kids and adults are overweight. They are **at risk** of obesity. They may develop worse weight problems as they get older.

Around the world, 300 million people are obese. More than 750 million are overweight. The World Health Organization (WHO) says obesity is a global **epidemic**. It is like a disease that is spreading everywhere. WHO names the problem "globesity." For the first time in history, more people in the world are overweight than hungry.

Scientists say that obesity has two

Which States Have the Most Obese Adults?

Where does your state rank?

Different U.S. states have different obesity rates. On this map, the states are ranked with numbers from 1 to 50. Mississippi, number 1, has the highest percentage of obese adults. Colorado, number 50, has the lowest.

NH 43

WA 29

VT 45

ME 32

MA 49

MT 45

ND 16

MN 25

NY 34

RI 48

OR 36

ID 37

WI 28

MI 6

PA 15

CT 47

SD 26

NJ 40

WY 42

IA 20

OH 13

DE 27

NV 32

UT 44

NE 20

IL 22

IN 9

WV 3

VA 22

DC 35

CA 31

CO 50

KS 22

MO 16

KY 6

NC 16

MD 29

TN 5

SC 10

AZ 40

NM 39

OK 14

AR 11

MS 1

AL 2

GA 12

TX 6

LA 4

FL 38

AK 19

HI
Not available

main causes. First, people are not active enough. Just 20 percent of Americans get enough exercise. Exercise burns **calories**, the units of energy that come from food. Calories that are not worked off are stored as fat instead.

Second, people eat too much. Americans and Canadians take in about 400 to 500 calories more than they need each day. They also eat too much of the wrong kinds of food. Their calories come from food that is high in fat and sugar. All over the world, more people are eating fast food. They eat junk food. They drink sodas. People become overweight, and that is not healthy.

CHAPTER TWO

LIVING IN THE DANGER ZONE

*Severely obese people such as this woman are
prone to many health problems.*

Obesity is harmful to human health. It raises the risk of getting many diseases. Heavy people can be at risk for asthma, arthritis, diabetes, heart disease, high blood pressure, and sleep disorders.

Ann Kobs was overweight for most of her life. By the time she was 58 years old, she weighed 320 pounds (145 kg). Throughout her life, she tried many different diets. Sometimes she lost weight, but she always gained it back again. She began to have health problems. She developed diabetes. This meant that her body could not produce enough **insulin** to handle the sugar in her body. Food is broken down into sugar in the body. Insulin helps the

Diabetes, high blood pressure, and increased risk of heart attack are just a few of the problems that the severely obese may develop.

blood sugar feed all the body's **cells**. Without enough insulin, Kobs's cells couldn't get enough sugar. The sugar in her blood was dangerously high. Kobs also had high blood pressure. It put her at risk for a stroke or a heart attack. She got out of breath when she walked. She had **sleep apnea** and stopped breathing many times each night. Kobs was so unhealthy that she thought she was going to die. *no really*

Bill Blohm was even sicker than Kobs. He was 44 years old and weighed 535 pounds (243 kg). His heart was failing. He gasped for breath when he tried to do anything at all.

His doctor told him he would die if he didn't change his life and lose weight.

Obesity can kill, but it also makes people very unhappy. They can't do the things other people can do. They are laughed at and teased. Richard Simmons, for instance, was an overweight child. In eighth grade, he weighed 200 pounds (90 kg). He couldn't play games or sports. He didn't have many friends. He hated himself and wished he could be like other people. When he grew up, he decided something had to change.

CHAPTER THREE

UNDOING OBESITY

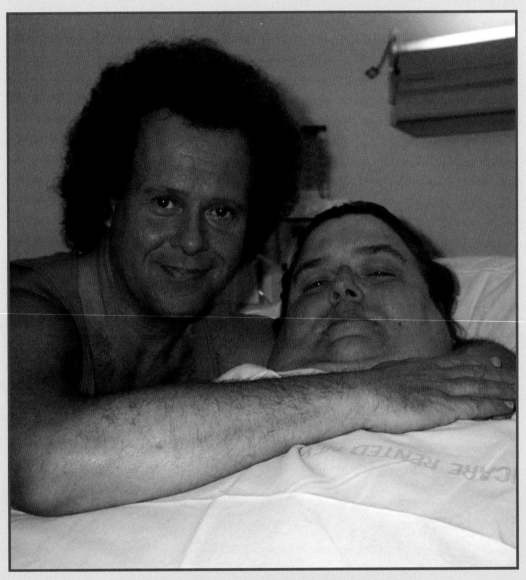

Michael Hebranko weighed 1100 pounds (400 kg) when he was hospitalized for his obesity. Fitness guru Richard Simmons (left) tries to inspire Hebranko to lose weight.

It's very hard to undo obesity. It takes willpower and hard work. You have to exercise. You have to learn to eat small servings of healthy foods, like fruits and vegetables. When you succeed, you can save your life.

Ann Kobs couldn't control her eating with willpower alone. She needed help, so she had **bariatric surgery**. A surgeon reshaped her stomach into a tiny pouch the size of a walnut. It could hold very little food. Then the hard part began. Kobs had to give up sodas, sugar, pasta, bread, and all junk foods. If she cheated, she would throw up. She had to learn to chew each bite of food 20 or 30 times. She could eat only half a cup of healthy food at a time. But Kobs was happy because she was not hungry. In less than two years, she lost 175 pounds (79 kg). Today, her diabetes and high blood pressure have gone away. She doesn't have sleep apnea anymore. She feels great and has lots of energy.

Life & Career Skills

A young person generally needs about 1500 to 2000 calories per day. (Active people burn more calories than couch potatoes.) Counting snacks, each meal should contain fewer than about 500 calories. See if you can select a fast food meal of 500 calories or less from the list below. You can mix and match from different restaurants but make a selection from each numbered group.

1. Burger King Whopper Junior with cheese [450 calories]
   Dairy Queen cheeseburger [340 calories]
   KFC extra-crispy chicken wings [190 calories]
   McDonald's 4-piece Chicken McNuggets
     [190 calories]
   Pizza Hut Thin 'n Crispy Crust cheese pizza, one slice
     [243 calories]
2. Burger King small hash brown round [240 calories]
   Hardee's cole slaw [240 calories]
   McDonald's medium French fries [450 calories]
   Popeye's onion rings [310 calories]
   Wendy's broccoli and cheese baked potato
     [470 calories]
3. Burger King small chocolate shake [390 calories]
   Carl's Jr. strawberries drink [400 calories]
   Dairy Queen small chocolate malt [650 calories]
   McDonald's medium Coca-Cola Classic [210 calories]
How'd you do?

Bill Blohm didn't have surgery for his weight problem. Instead, he changed his lifestyle. He gave up all junk food and ate mostly high-protein foods such as lean meats and fish. He joined a gym and exercised five days a week. At first he swam. As he got stronger, he began lifting weights. Working out became Blohm's

Crystal Kaprowicz and her father John both underwent surgery to implant a flexible band that squeezes their stomach. This band prevents them from overeating. Both show the weight loss that they achieved from the surgery.

new way of life. In two years, he lost 200 pounds (90 kg), but best of all, his heart grew strong and healthy. He says exercise saved his life.

Richard Simmons changed his lifestyle, too. He decided it was time to learn to love his body. He changed his diet and ate only small amounts of healthy food. He exercised hard every day. Simmons became a fitness expert. Now, he teaches others to learn to like themselves and lose weight.

So fake

CHAPTER FOUR

IN THE PUBLIC INTEREST

A girl enjoys fresh fruit. Many schools have been changing their menus in an effort to reduce fatty foods.

Today's young people are at risk for an obese future. Many kids eat too much junk food and don't like healthy foods. Many don't exercise regularly. Obesity is such a bad problem that schools and communities are getting involved to change everyone's lifestyle.

At Excelsior Middle School in San Francisco, California, students grow their own gardens. They raise lettuce, beets, carrots, onions, beans, herbs, and much more. They harvest their vegetables, prepare fresh salads, and serve them in the cafeteria. The students enjoy the healthy salad bars. Gardening helps the students learn about nutrition, too. They learn that vegetables are low in

*Eating more fruits and vegetables and less processed
food can be one way to stay fit and lean.*

calories and high in vitamins. They define junk food as

lots of empty calories from fats and sugars that don't build

healthy bodies.

In Oakland, California, Nora Cody teaches elementary classes about nutrition. Her students learn to read food labels. They read how much sugar is in a can of soda. Then they measure out that much sugar in teaspoons. They rub fast foods on paper bags to see how much grease rubs off.

When people understand nutrition, they are more likely to change their lifestyles. At Lick-Wilmerding High School in San Francisco, California , the cafeteria banned cookies and muffins. Now the school offers granola bars and fruit instead. Everywhere in California, soda machines are banned in schools.

This school in Northport, New York, promotes fitness classes in which everyone can participate. Kids who don't play traditional sports such as football or basketball are not left out.

Healthy food prevents obesity, and so does exercise. At South Middle School in Morgantown, West Virginia, gym class combines exercise and fun. Students play the popular video game Dance Dance Revolution. Gym students dance on interactive mats. They have to think fast and work out to win. In Manitoba, Canada, physical education is now required for all 11th- and 12th-grade students. Young people who exercise aren't likely to become overweight adults.

CHAPTER FIVE

THE ROLE OF SCIENCE

*A mother and daughter have similar body fat
ratios. Obesity often runs in families.*

Life & Career Skills

Check out your school's menu options for a typical day. See if the choices include protein (meat or dairy), starches (potatoes, rice, pasta), and fruit or vegetables. See if you can put together a meal that fits the Food Pyramid recommendations.

Consider healthy portion sizes, too:

Grains: ½ cup (113 g); equal to about half a tennis ball.

Fruits: ½ cup (113 g); another half tennis ball.

Meat or fish: 3 or 4 ounces (85 to 113 g); the size of a computer mouse.

Cheese: 1 ounce (28 g); about the size of your thumb.

Low fat milk: 1 cup (227 g); equal to a whole tennis ball.

Any size vegetable serving is OK as long as it doesn't include butter, oils, or other fats.

You can control portion size yourself, but if your school menu includes too many high-fat foods, talk to your parents, teachers, and principal about changing the school diet.

Scientists want to know why so many young people are overweight. They study how being overweight affects kids when they grow up.

Overweight kids are at risk of becoming obese adults. Scientists have learned that these kids have more fat cells than slim kids. Unused calories from food are stored in the body as fat cells. The more empty calories you eat and don't use, the more fat cells multiply. Kids who are overweight can have three times more fat cells than kids of normal weight. Their bodies have learned to store more fat. The fat cells can get smaller, but they never go away. They are there for life. They make it easier to gain weight and harder to lose weight in the future. That's why scientists say it is better to prevent obesity than to try to undo it.

Scientists believe that young people learn to eat too many calories from their families. Scientists have studied how families eat. In their studies, they've found that children learn to like what their parents teach them to eat at home. If kids are raised on unhealthy foods, they keep eating the same foods as adults. Family habits have to change so young people grow up to enjoy healthy foods.

21st Century Content

Jane Wardle is an expert on obesity in young people. Here are some of her tips for kids to help prevent obesity.

1. Clean plates are not important. Only eat till you aren't hungry anymore.

2. Wait a few minutes before asking for second helpings. Give the brain's appetite center some time to get the full signal from your stomach.

3. Choose healthy foods most of the time. But sweets and fatty foods are OK sometimes. Don't try to give up your favorite foods completely!

*Studies show that the families that play together
are healthier and less prone to obesity.*

Scientists also study why people get hungry. Hunger signals come from a special area in the brain. It's called the appetite center. If you're overweight, the appetite center might not work well. Your brain might not be getting good signals that you are full. Some scientists are trying to develop new medicines that control hunger signals. Others are trying to create drugs that stop the body from storing fat calories. Someday drugs like these might prevent weight gain, but for now, experts say lifestyle changes are needed to save people from an obese world.

GLOSSARY

at risk in danger; to have an increased chance

bariatric surgery (bare ee AT rik SUHR juh ree) surgery on the stomach and/or intestines to help very obese people lose weight. There are several different operations, such as gastric bypass surgery or lap banding. Bariatrics is the medical study and treatment of obesity.

calories (KAL uh reez) units of measurement of the energy in food

cells (selz) the basic building blocks of living things. The human body is made of trillions of cells.

epidemic (ep ih DEM ick) a fast-spreading disease or health problem that affects a large number of people at the same time

insulin (IN suh lin) a chemical made by the body that helps move sugar from the blood into the cells, so it can be turned into energy

lifestyle (LIFE stile) way of living, including diet, exercise, activity, and habits

obese (oh BEESS) an excess of body fat that is harmful to health, usually 20 to 30 percent over normal weight

overweight (OH vur wate) weighing more than the ideal, healthy weight but not obese

sleep apnea (SLEEP AP nee uh) in which a person stops breathing for several seconds at a time

21st CENTURY SKILLS LIBRARY

FOR MORE INFORMATION

Books

Daly, Melissa, and Sylvie Boutaudou. *Weighing In: How to Understand Your Body, Lose Weight, and Live a Healthier Lifestyle.* London: Amulet Books for Middle Grade and Young Adults, 2006.

DK Publishing. *My Food Pyramid.* New York: DK Children, 2007.

DK Publishing. *Kids' Fun and Healthy Cookbook.* New York: DK Children, 2007.

Web Sites

BaM: Body and Mind, Food and Nutrition, Centers for Disease Control and Prevention
www.bam.gov/sub_foodnutrition/index.html
Nutrition facts, games, recipes, and activities for kids from the U.S. government

Food Guides for Canada and the United States
www.stemnet.nf.ca/CITE/food-guides.htm
Gives kids a rainbow guide to healthy eating and tips about tasty foods to try

Kidnetic.com
www.kidnetic.com
A site dedicated to bodies, food, fitness, and fun

Kids' Health
www.cyh.com/SubDefault.aspx?p=255
Follow the Your Body and Your Food links to What Is Obesity?, Fast Food, Food Labels, and many more topics

"Packing Fat," Science News for Kids
www.sciencenewsforkids.org/articles/20041027/Feature1.asp
Discusses overweight in kids and some of the reasons why it is a problem

INDEX

ABOUT THE AUTHOR

Toney Allman holds degrees from Ohio State University and the University of Hawaii. She lives in rural Virginia, where she enjoys gardening, reading, and learning about the natural world. She has written more than two dozen nonfiction books for students and learned something new and fun from each and every one of them.